HAL•LEONARD
INSTRUMENTAL
PLAY-ALONG

AUDIO
ACCESS
INCLUDED

PLAYBACK+
Pitch • Balance • Loop

ALTO SAX
12 HOT SINGLES

Audio arrangements by Peter Deneff

To access audio visit:
www.halleonard.com/mylibrary

Enter Code
5905-1325-2484-2188

ISBN 978-1-5400-5890-4

HAL•LEONARD®

Visit Hal Leonard Online at
www.halleonard.com

Contact us:
Hal Leonard
7777 West Bluemound Road
Milwaukee, WI 53213
Email: info@halleonard.com

In Europe, contact:
Hal Leonard Europe Limited
42 Wigmore Street
Marylebone, London, W1U 2RN
Email: info@halleonardeurope.com

In Australia, contact:
Hal Leonard Australia Pty. Ltd.
4 Lentara Court
Cheltenham, Victoria, 3192 Australia
Email: info@halleonard.com.au

CONTENTS

4 **Broken** .... lovelytheband

6 **Havana** .... Camila Cabello & Young Thug

8 **Heaven** .... Kane Brown

10 **High Hopes** ....Panic! At the Disco

5 **The Middle** .... Zedd, Maren Morris & Grey

12 **Natural** .... Imagine Dragons

13 **No Place Like You** .... Backstreet Boys

14 **Shallow** .... Lady Gaga & Bradley Cooper

15 **Sucker** .... Jonas Brothers

16 **Sunflower** .... Post Malone & Swae Lee

20 **Thank U, Next** .... Ariana Grande

18 **Youngblood** .... 5 Seconds of Summer

BROKEN

ALTO SAX

Words and Music by MITCHELL COLLINS
CHRISTIAN MEDICE and SAMANTHA DeROSA

THE MIDDLE

ALTO SAX

Words and Music by SARAH AARONS,
MARCUS LOMAX, JORDAN JOHNSON,
ANTON ZASLAVSKI, KYLE TREWARTHA,
MICHAEL TREWARTHA and STEFAN JOHNSON

HAVANA

ALTO SAX

Words and Music by CAMILA CABELLO, LOUIS BELL,
PHARRELL WILLIAMS, ADAM FEENEY, ALI TAMPOSI,
JEFFERY LAMAR WILLIAMS, BRIAN LEE, ANDREW WOTMAN,
BRITTANY HAZZARD and KAAN GUNESBERK

HEAVEN

ALTO SAX

Words and Music by SHY CARTER,
LINDSAY RIMES and MATTHEW McGINN

To Coda ⊕

D.S. al Coda

mf

CODA
⊕

mf

f

mf

HIGH HOPES

ALTO SAX

Words and Music by BRENDON URIE,
SAMUEL HOLLANDER, WILLIAM LOBBAN BEAN,
JONAS JEBERG, JACOB SINCLAIR,
JENNY OWEN YOUNGS, ILSEY JUBER,
LAUREN PRITCHARD and TAYLOR PARKS

NATURAL

ALTO SAX

Words and Music by DAN REYNOLDS,
WAYNE SERMON, BEN McKEE,
DANIEL PLATZMAN, JUSTIN TRANTOR,
MATTIAS LARSSON and ROBIN FREDRICKSSON

NO PLACE LIKE YOU

ALTO SAX

Words and Music by TROY VERGES,
BRETT JAMES and JOSHUA MILLER

SHALLOW

from A STAR IS BORN

ALTO SAX

Words and Music by STEFANI GERMANOTTA,
MARK RONSON, ANDREW WYATT
and ANTHONY ROSSOMANDO

SUCKER

ALTO SAX

Words and Music by NICK JONAS,
JOSEPH JONAS, CARL ROSEN,
RYAN TEDDER, LOUIS BELL,
ADAM FEENEY and KEVIN JONAS

SUNFLOWER

from SPIDER-MAN: INTO THE SPIDER-VERSE

ALTO SAX

Words and Music by AUSTIN RICHARD POST,
CARL AUSTIN ROSEN, KHALIF BROWN,
CARTER LANG, LOUIS BELL
and BILLY WALSH

YOUNGBLOOD

ALTO SAX

Words and Music by ASHTON IRWIN
CALUM HOOD, LOUIS BELL
LUKE HEMMING, ALEXANDRA TAMPOSI
and ANDREW WATT

19

THANK U, NEXT

ALTO SAX

Words and Music by ARIANA GRANDE,
VICTORIA McCANTS, KIMBERLY KRYSIUK
TAYLA PARX, TOMMY BROWN,
CHARLES ANDERSON and MICHAEL FOSTER